Riffs, Ch...

▶▶ *FastForward*™

Blues Guitar Improvisation

with Andy Jones

Wise Publications
London / New York / Sydney / Paris / Copenhagen / Madrid

Exclusive Distributors:
Music Sales Limited
8/9 Frith Street, London W1V 5TZ, England.
Music Sales Pty Limited
120 Rothschild Avenue, Rosebery, NSW 2018, Australia.
Music Sales Corporation
257 Park Avenue South, New York, NY10010,
United States of America.

Order No.AM953260
ISBN 0-7119-7447-2
This book © Copyright 1999 by Wise Publications.

Edited and arranged by Andy Jones.
Music processed by Paul Ewers Music Design.
Cover photography by George Taylor.

Text photographs courtesy of
London Features International.

Printed and bound in the United Kingdom.

Your Guarantee of Quality:
As publishers, we strive to produce every book to
the highest commercial standards.
The music has been freshly engraved and the book has
been carefully designed to minimise awkward page turns
and to make playing from it a real pleasure.
Particular care has been given to specifying acid-free,
neutral-sized paper made from pulps which have not
been elemental chlorine bleached.
This pulp is from farmed sustainable forests and
was produced with special regard for the environment.
Throughout, the printing and binding have
been planned to ensure a sturdy, attractive publication
which should give years of enjoyment.
If your copy fails to meet our high standards, please
inform us and we will gladly replace it.

Music Sales' complete catalogue describes
thousands of titles and is available in full colour sections
by subject, direct from Music Sales Limited.
Please state your areas of interest and send a cheque/postal
order for £1.50 for postage to: Music Sales Limited,
Newmarket Road, Bury St. Edmunds, Suffolk IP33 3YB.

www.internetmusicshop.com

Guitar Tablature Explained

Guitar music can be notated three different ways: on a musical stave, in tablature, and in rhythm slashes

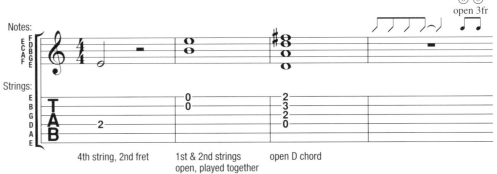

RHYTHM SLASHES are written above the stave. Strum chords in the rhythm indicated. Round noteheads indicate single notes.

THE MUSICAL STAVE shows pitches and rhythms and is divided by lines into bars. Pitches are named after the first seven letters of the alphabet.

TABLATURE graphically represents the guitar fingerboard. Each horizontal line represents a string, and each number represents a fret.

4th string, 2nd fret 1st & 2nd strings open, played together open D chord

definitions for special guitar notation

SEMI-TONE BEND: Strike the note and bend up a semi-tone (1/2 step).

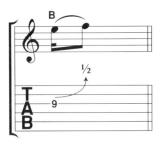

WHOLE-TONE BEND: Strike the note and bend up a whole-tone (whole step).

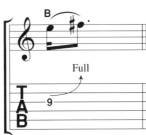

GRACE NOTE BEND: Strike the note and bend as indicated. Play the first note as quickly as possible.

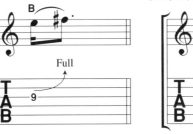

QUARTER-TONE BEND: Strike the note and bend up a 1/4 step.

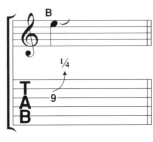

BEND & RELEASE: Strike the note and bend up as indicated, then release back to the original note.

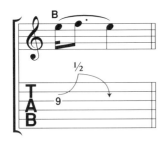

COMPOUND BEND & RELEASE: Strike the note and bend up and down in the rhythm indicated.

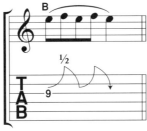

PRE-BEND: Bend the note as indicated, then strike it.

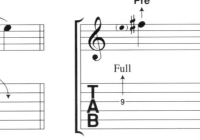

PRE-BEND & RELEASE: Bend the note as indicated. Strike it and release the note back to the original pitch.

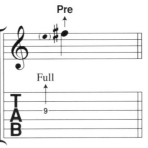

UNISON BEND: Strike the two notes simultaneously and bend the lower note up to the pitch of the higher.

BEND & RESTRIKE: Strike the note and bend as indicated then restrike the string where the symbol occurs.

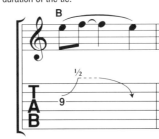

BEND, HOLD AND RELEASE: Same as bend and release but hold the bend for the duration of the tie.

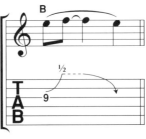

BEND AND TAP: Bend the note as indicated and tap the higher fret while still holding the bend.

VIBRATO: The string is vibrated by rapidly bending and releasing the note with the fretting hand.

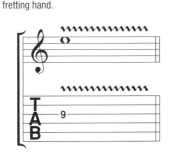

HAMMER-ON: Strike the first (lower) note with one finger, then sound the higher note (on the same string) with another finger by fretting it without picking.

PULL-OFF: Place both fingers on the notes to be sounded, Strike the first note and without picking, pull the finger off to sound the second (lower) note.

LEGATO SLIDE (GLISS): Strike the first note and then slide the same fret-hand finger up or down to the second note. The second note is not struck.

NOTE: The speed of any bend is indicated by the music notation and tempo.

SHIFT SLIDE (GLISS & RESTRIKE): Same as legato slide, except the second note is struck.

TRILL: Very rapidly alternate between the notes indicated by continuously hammering on and pulling off.

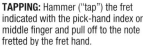

TAPPING: Hammer ("tap") the fret indicated with the pick-hand index or middle finger and pull off to the note fretted by the fret hand.

PICK SCRAPE: The edge of the pick is rubbed down (or up) the string, producing a scratchy sound.

MUFFLED STRINGS: A percussive sound is produced by laying the fret hand across the string(s) without depressing, and striking them with the pick hand.

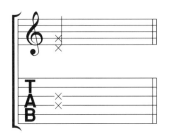

NATURAL HARMONIC: Strike the note while the fret-hand lightly touches the string directly over the fret indicated.

PINCH HARMONIC: The note is fretted normally and a harmonic is produced by adding the edge of the thumb or the tip of the index finger of the pick hand to the normal pick attack.

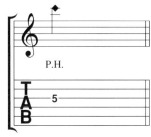

HARP HARMONIC: The note is fretted normally and a harmonic is produced by gently resting the pick hand's index finger directly above the indicated fret (in parentheses) while the pick hand's thumb or pick assists by plucking the appropriate string.

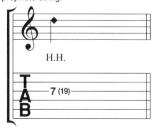

PALM MUTING: The note is partially muted by the pick hand lightly touching the string(s) just before the bridge.

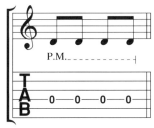

RAKE: Drag the pick across the strings indicated with a single motion.

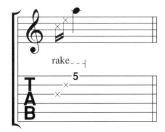

TREMOLO PICKING: The note is picked as rapidly and continuously as possible.

ARPEGGIATE: Play the notes of the chord indicated by quickly rolling them from bottom to top.

SWEEP PICKING: Rhythmic downstroke and/or upstroke motion across the strings.

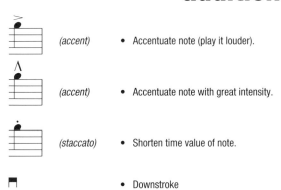

VIBRATO DIVE BAR AND RETURN: The pitch of the note or chord is dropped a specific number of steps (in rhythm) then returned to the original pitch.

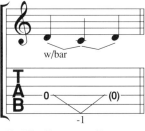

VIBRATO BAR SCOOP: Depress the bar just before striking the note, then quickly release the bar.

VIBRATO BAR DIP: Strike the note and then immediately drop a specific number of steps, then release back to the original pitch.

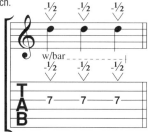

additional musical definitions

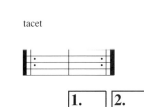	(accent)	• Accentuate note (play it louder).
Λ	(accent)	• Accentuate note with great intensity.
⠁	(staccato)	• Shorten time value of note.
⊓		• Downstroke
V		• Upstroke

D.%. al Coda

D.C. al Fine

tacet

• Go back to the sign (%), then play until the bar marked *To Coda* ⊕ then skip to the section marked ⊕ *Coda*.

• Go back to the beginning of the song and play until the bar marked *Fine* (end).

• Instrument is silent (drops out).

• Repeat bars between signs.

• When a repeated section has different endings, play the first ending only the first time and the second ending only the second time.

► **B.B. KING**

"The blues are almost sacred to some people, but others don't understand and when I can't make them understand it makes me feel bad because they mean so much to me."

Introduction

Hello, and welcome to ▶▶**Fast**_Forward_

Congratulations on purchasing a product that will improve your playing and provide you with hours of pleasure. All the music in this book has been specially created by professional musicians to give you maximum value and enjoyment.

If you already know how to 'drive' your instrument, but you'd like to do a little customising, you've pulled in at the right place. We'll put you on the fast track to playing the kinds of riffs and patterns that today's professionals rely on.

We'll provide you with a vocabulary of riffs that you can apply in a wide variety of musical situations, with a special emphasis on giving you the techniques that will help you in a band situation.

This book will teach you how to create your own classic blues solos, from just a couple of classic blues scales. In fact, the blues scale forms the basis for every solo in the book, which are all based on the traditional blues chord sequence. Each section will introduce you to a different style of blues playing - all of which use the same basic techniques.

All the music examples in this book come with full-band audio tracks so that you get your chance to join in - all exercises are demonstrated at full speed and at a slower practice speed. Practise and learn the examples and then take off on your own over the backing tracks!

All players and bands get their sounds and styles by drawing on the same basic building blocks. With ▶▶**Fast**_Forward_ you'll quickly learn these, and then be ready to use them to create your own style.

TRACK1 Tuning Notes

▶▶ *ERIC CLAPTON*
"Otis Rush, Buddy Guy ...it's not so much technique that I listen for;
it's the content really, and the feeling and the tone."

Eric's Dominoes
Blues Scale Shapes

Our first tune is a rocky blues groove in the style of Eric Clapton. Check out the rhythm guitar pattern - it's something of a set piece.

The very first thing you're going to have to get to grips with are the basic scale shapes. Your first blues is in G, so listed below are three basic blues scales that you can use in that key.

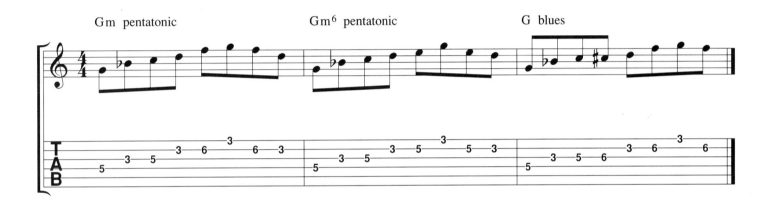

G minor pentatonic is a simple scale to start with - it only has five notes, giving it a very distinctively blues sound. The minor 6th pentatonic is an interesting sound combining the

bluesy minor 3rd and the natural 6th. The third scale is a classic - the blues scale - some blues players never use anything else!

TRACKS 2+3

Track 2 demonstrates the patterns slowly - take some time to work out the fingering of these basic scales and then try playing along with Track 3.

TRACKS 4+5

Track 4 demonstrates the same patterns at full speed - when you're feeling confident try playing along with Track 5.

Chord Tones

As well as scale patterns, a good blues player will also be aware of the important chord tones in the blues sequence. The example below gives you all the chord tones for a blues in the key of G.

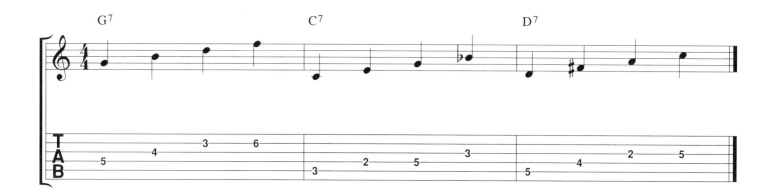

Track 6 demonstrates these patterns slowly - familiarise yourself with the shapes on the fretboard and then play along slowly with Track 7.

Now listen to Track 8, which demonstrates the chord tones at full speed, and then try playing along with the backing on Track 9.

These patterns and shapes are going to provide the raw material for your solo, so make sure you practise them until you are absolutely confident.

Pentatonic Scale Patterns

Now, we're going to take these patterns and create some classic blues phrases. The example below is a simple but effective pattern based on the G minor pentatonic scale.

Gm pentatonic (over G⁷ blues)

TRACKS 10+11

Track 10 is a slow version of this pattern, and Track 11 is the backing. Take your time with this one and you'll nail it!

Experimenting with this kind of shape adds detail to your solos. If you don't want to be one of those guys (or gals) irritating the music store manager on Saturday afternoon, cultivate this kind of informed playing - widdling will get you nowhere!

Pentatonic Blues Phrases

The next example takes these shapes a step further and creates some genuine blues lines. Practise these patterns really slowly, and then build up the tempo gradually.

Listen carefully to Track 12 and take note of the rhythmic patterns - a lot of blues parts can look fearsome when written out, but make perfect sense if you just listen! Track 13 is your chance to play this part over a slow backing.

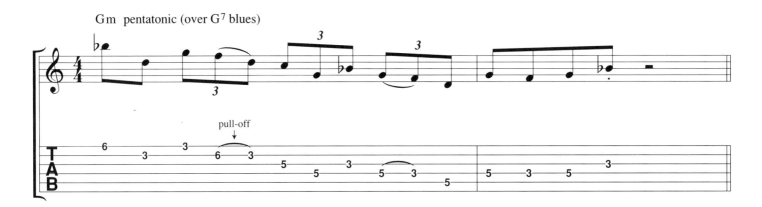

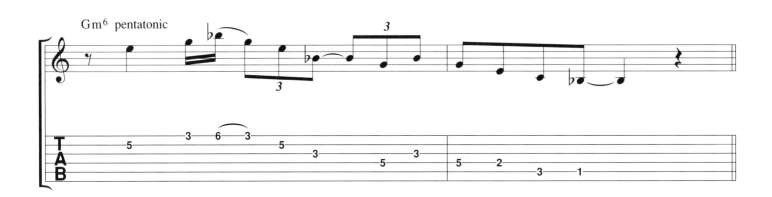

This is what the part sounds like at full speed!
Have a go yourself over the backing on Track 15.

Experiment with these shapes and scales, but
always try to play rhythmically - there's nothing
more boring than endless streams of continuous
motion, so try to give your solo breathing space -
don't be afraid to leave gaps!

▶▶Spotlight On Techniques

Pull Offs:-

This example makes extensive use of the pull-off
technique (see bars 1, 3 & 5), which is an
important part of blues playing. There's a
tendency to rush the second note in each pair so
isolate each pull-off and practise slowly.

Bends:-

This device is vital to blues phrasing - check out
the semitone bend in the last bar of this example.
When you practise, try to get this bend in tune -
it will need a little work.

▶▶ *JIMI HENDRIX*
"You can have your own blues. Folk blues are not necessarily the only type of blues in the world... Everybody has some kind of blues to offer, you know."

Take A Solo

Here's your first chance to try your hand at a complete solo - 'Eric's Dominoes'.

Written out below is an example of a solo that you might play over this type of blues - note that it sounds like an improvisation - which is exactly what it is - I took a few passes at a solo and chose this one! Listen to Track 16 and try to visualise the shapes on the fretboard as you listen - note that rather than a count-in, the backing starts with a drum fill.

Track 17 is the backing track - you can try to play the solo as tabbed out over the page or you could use some of the ideas above and improvise your own part. The backing track cycles through the blues sequence a couple more times than Track 16, so there's plenty of time for you to try out your own ideas.

▶▶Spotlight On Techniques

Sliding:-
Another useful technique is sliding into a note (see bars 4 & 6). Slides will give you a different sound to a hammer-on or pull off, adding variety to your solo.

Double Stops:-
Double stops add harmonic weight to your solos (see bar 10). If you use double stops in a trio setting, with drums and bass, they can help to outline the harmony and make the band sound fuller.

Eric's Dominoes

TRACKS 16+17

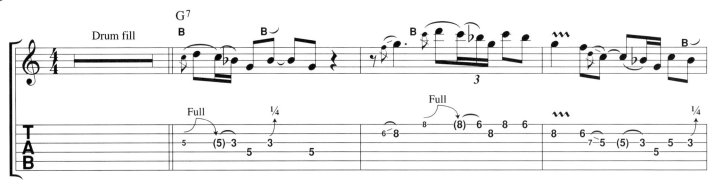

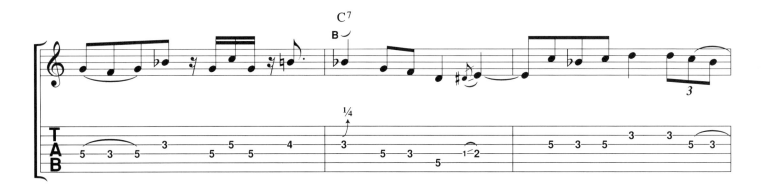

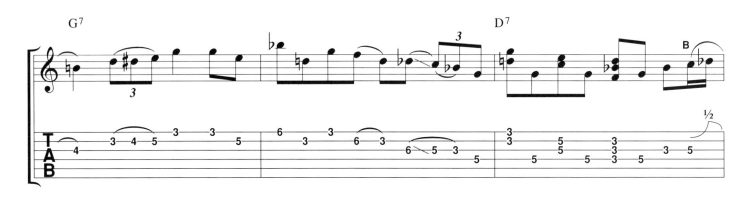

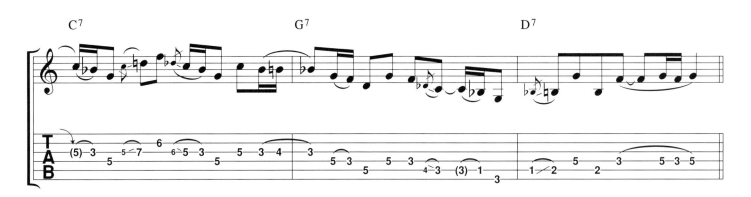

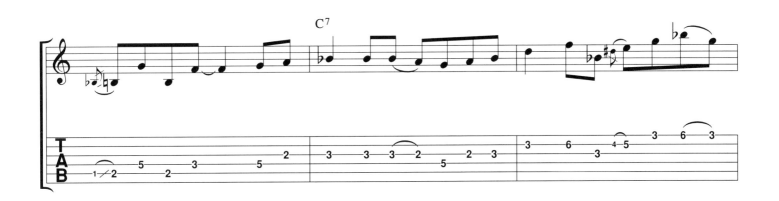

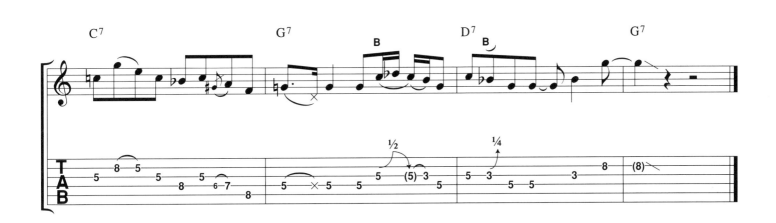

▶▶ *ALBERT COLLINS*
"I tried using picks two or three times, man. I just don't like picks...
Picks will make you fast, though. But I really like digging in with my fingers."

The Iceman Cometh

This chapter is concerned with another style of blues - in fact it's based on the playing of Albert Collins.

Here's a typical rhythm guitar part in his style - you'll learn the lead guitar part later in this chapter.

TRACKS 18+19

The Dominant 7 Blues Scale

This tune, like the previous one, is a blues in G, using the basic chords of G^7, C^7 and D^7. Here are some simple scale options for this tune - listen to Track 20 and then practise slowly with the backing on Track 21.

TRACKS 20+21

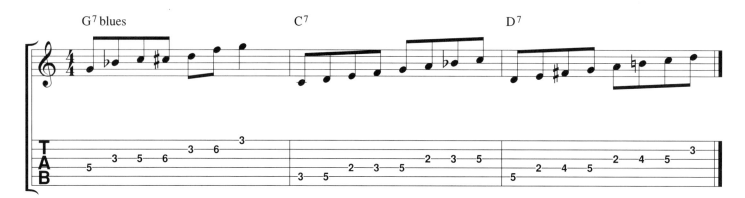

TRACKS 22+23

Track 22 demonstrates these patterns up to speed - try playing them yourself along with Track 23.

Chord Tones

The example below lists the essential chord tones for a blues in G. Although this may seem like an academic exercise, it's really a necessity - if you can't play the chord tones on a simple blues, don't venture onto a stage! Listen to the slow version on Track 24 and then try playing along with Track 25.

TRACKS 24+25

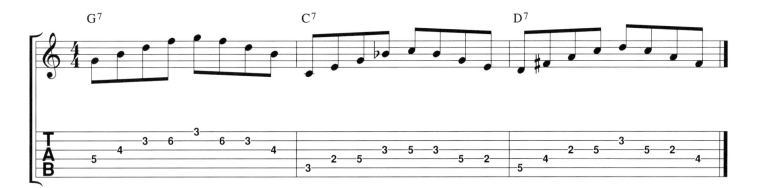

TRACKS 26+27

Once you're happy with these shapes, try speeding them up! Listen to Track 26 and then play along with Track 27.

Rhythm Patterns

The next example will help you to get accustomed to the swinging feel of this type of blues - each beat of the bar is divided into three triplets. You should always feel the triplet even when you're playing what looks like straight quavers on paper! Try slowly at first...

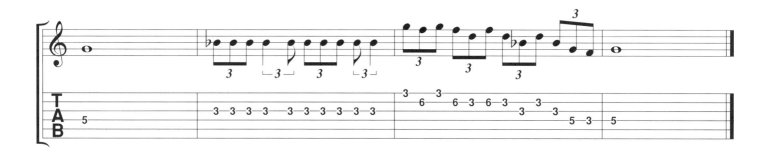

... and then check out the faster example on Track 30. Track 31 is the backing track for you to practise over.

▶▶Spotlight On Techniques

Triplets:-

This whole piece has a swinging triplet feel so naturally the guitar solo makes heavy use of this subdivision - try to keep them even and flowing.

Wing It!

Here's your chance to play the full solo - once you've mastered the solo as tabbed out below, experiment with some of the ideas and shapes and improvise your own solo over the backing track.

The solo guitar plays in the gaps left by the rest of the band - a very dramatic effect using lots of high bends and wailing held notes, until eventually the band kicks into a steadier groove. This solo goes quite high up the neck - don't worry, just practise slowly and BE PATIENT!

▶▶Spotlight On Techniques

Use Of Higher Register:-
The solo begins with a dramatic statement played way up the neck. The screaming high note is an immediate call to attention, and the fact that the second phrase is played much lower down the neck makes it sound like an "answer" to the first.

Double Stops:-
The bluesy phrase in bar 6 makes use of a double stop - again this adds fullness to your improvisation.

The Iceman Cometh

TRACKS 32+33

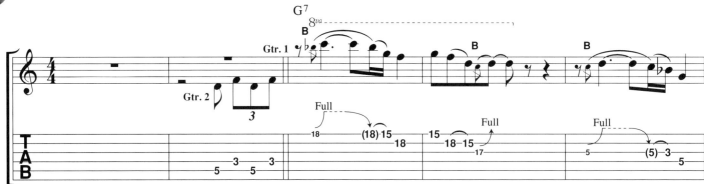

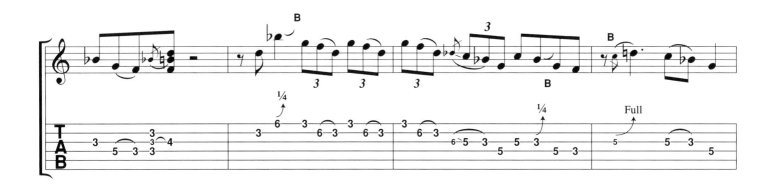

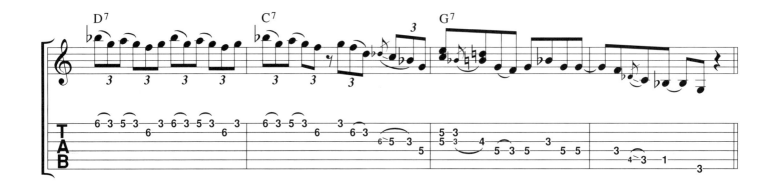

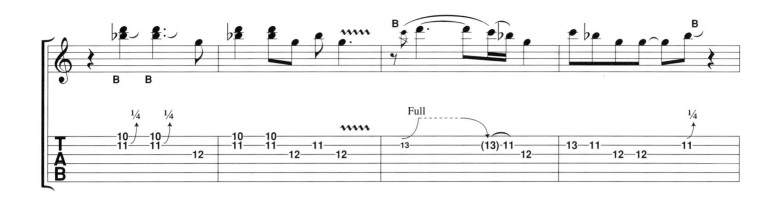

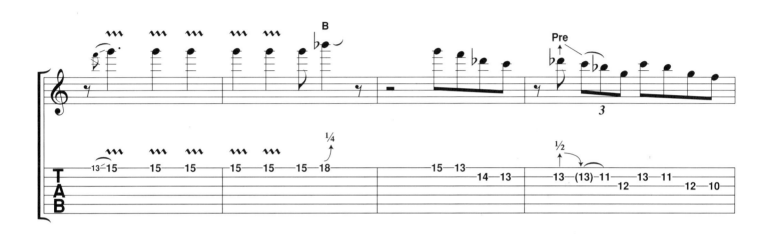

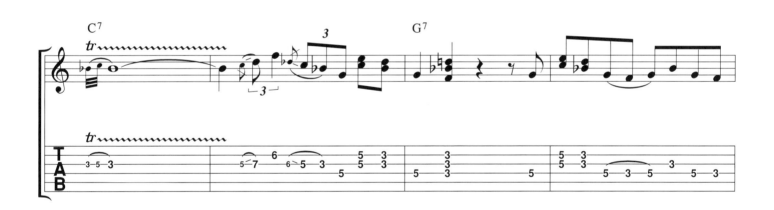

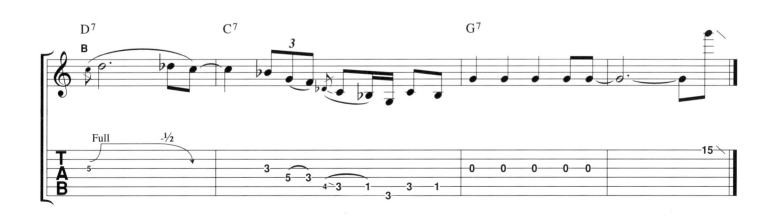

▶▶ STEVIE RAY VAUGHAN
*"When you listen to your heart it seems like you got something to say,
whether it be through music or through whatever, 'cause it's not all in your head.
It's got more to do with living it."*

One For Stevie Ray
12/8: The Slow Blues

In Chapter 3, we're going to explore another common blues format - the 12/8 slow blues. This differs from 4/4 in that the four beats of the bar are each divided into three quaver units (triplets). This gives a bouncy swinging feel.

Another element of this kind of blues is rhythmic freedom - all the great blues players play very freely over the 12/8 blues. This can result in music that looks very complicated - however, just listen to the demonstrations on the CD and you'll hear that all the phrases make perfect sense.

This first exercise shows some of the more common rhythms used in 12/8 blues. They're all played on one note so that you can focus all your concentration on understanding the rhythms. Start really slowly by listening to Track 34 and then try playing in time with Track 35.

 TRACKS 34+35

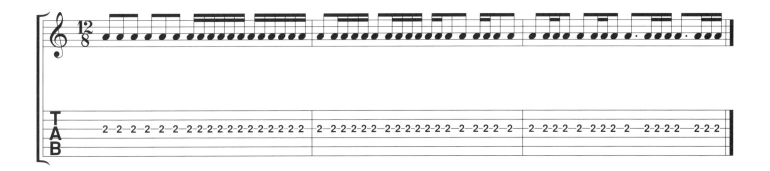

 TRACKS 36+37

Once you're confident with the subdivisions of the beat speed up and try playing along with Track 37.

Now that you're familiar with some 12/8 blues rhythms, let's introduce something for the left hand! The solo that we're working towards is a minor blues on A, so let's play slowly up the A minor blues scale, spending two beats on each note. The rhythm you're playing is exactly the same as in the example above.

TRACKS 38+39

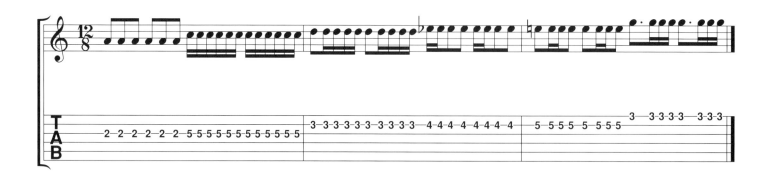

TRACKS 40+41

Now try the same exercise up to speed.

The next example doubles this rate of movement - you'll now only be spending one beat (3 quavers) on each note of the scale - and this time we're going up the scale and back down again.

TRACKS 42+43

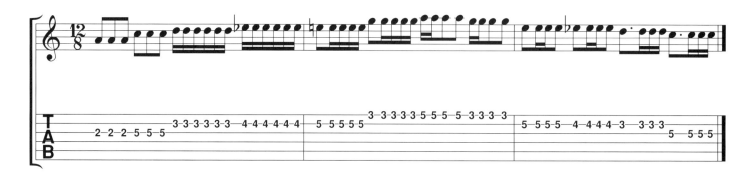

TRACKS 44+45

Once you've mastered this at the slower tempo, try bringing it up to speed.

Using The Blues Scale

If you've followed all the steps in this chapter, you should now be feeling more confident with these rhythms!

This last example shows a few simple lines which use the rhythms of the previous example - once again, they're all based on the A blues scale.

Here's the same example up to speed.

▶▶ *JOHNNY WINTER*
...Made his recording debut at the age of 16, and produced and arranged a series of acclaimed albums for Blues legend Muddy Waters.

▶ *JOHN LEE HOOKER*
"If you're playing blues, play with your heart and ears. The blues isn't in the book, you've got to feel it. If you don't have the feeling and rhythm, you can forget it."

Over To You

Here's a typical 12/8 minor blues solo, using some of the ideas we've just discussed. You can approach this in two ways: either learn the solo as tabbed out below, and play it over the backing track, or, pick out the sections that you like and create your own solo.

If this type of feel is new to you, just spend some time playing along with the track until you feel more comfortable with the basic pulse. The 12/8 blues offers great scope for improvisation and every player has their own approach to it.

▶▶Spotlight On Techniques

Hammer-ons/Pull-offs:-
Check out the second half of bar 2, this is something of a blues set piece!

Quarter Tone Bends:-
See bar 1 beat 4 - here we're bending the minor third up a quarter tone. This adds a certain ambiguity to the harmony - is it major or minor?

Repetitive Figures:-
Check out the last 2 bars - here a repetitive rhythm is used and the exact notes adjusted to fit the changing harmony. Using such figures makes your solos more cohesive and shows that you understand the chord changes!

One For Stevie Ray

TRACKS 50+51

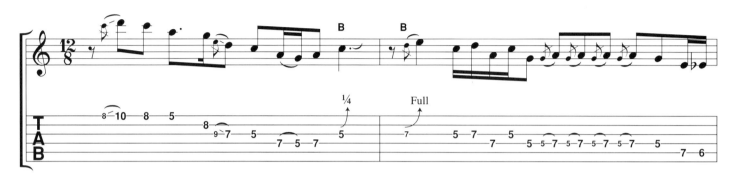

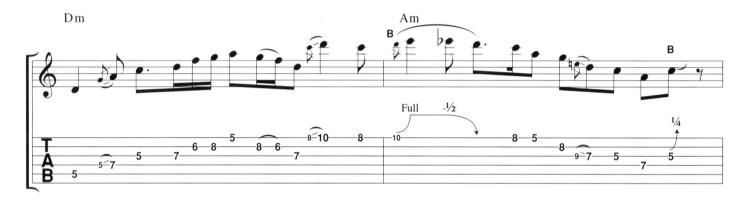

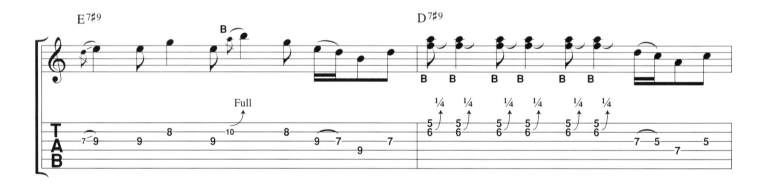

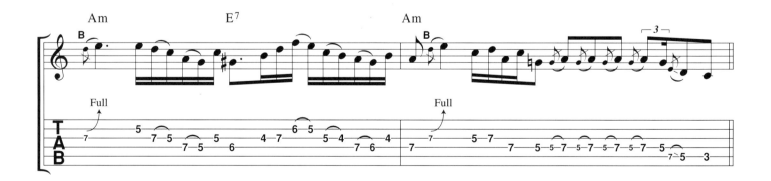

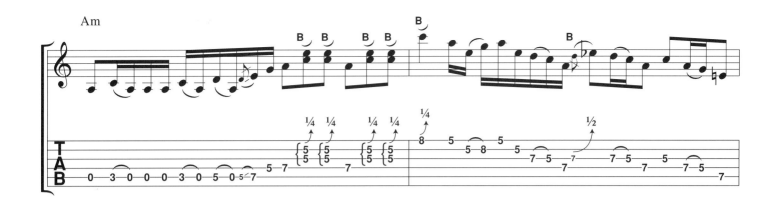

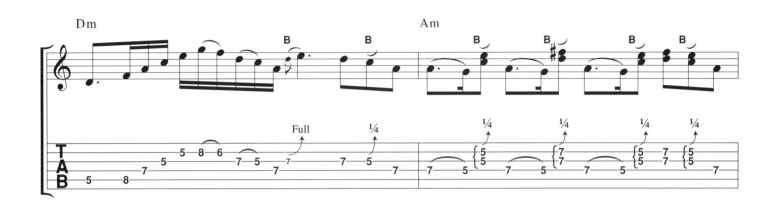

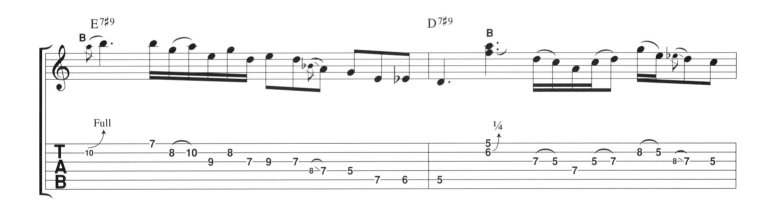

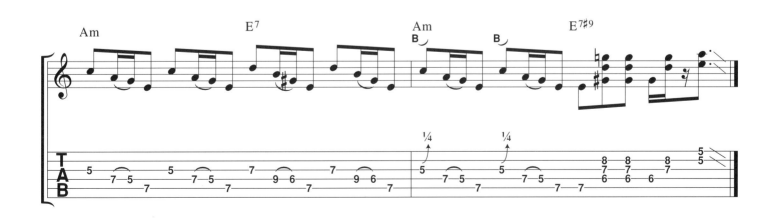

Robben's Bag
Rhumba Blues Scale Shapes

Our fourth tune ("Robben's Bag") is a rhumba blues - check out the distinctive drum pattern - it has a popular blues feel.

The piece is a simple blues in C - here are the scales you'll need to play over this progression. Try them slowly at first...

 TRACKS 52+53

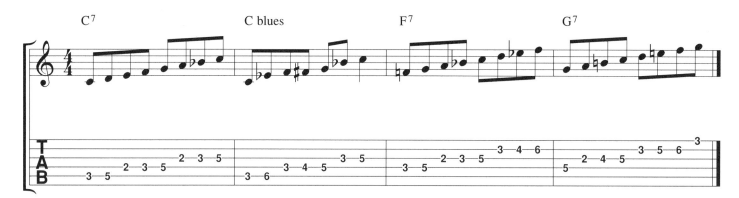

 TRACKS 54+55

... and then play them up to speed.

Chord Tones

Actually, the tonic blues scale, C blues in this case, can be used over both the I and IV chords in this song - C and F. Try to mix both approaches to these chords - playing just the blues scale with flattened third, over the I chord, can obscure the chord movement to the IV chord.

Here are the basic arpeggios for this blues. Once again they're based around chords I, IV and V - in the key of C, they are C7, F7 and G7. Practise them slowly...

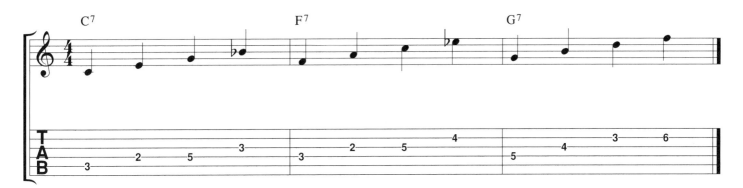

TRACKS 56+57

TRACKS 58+59

... and build up your tempo until you can play along with Track 59.

Using 7th Arpeggios

The next example illustrates ascending and descending 7th arpeggios that fit this tune. Arpeggios like these will help to fill out the harmony when you're just playing in a trio (with bass and drums) without keyboards.

The second half of the example is an arpeggio shape which includes both the sixth and seventh degrees of the scales. The sixth degree is a colour tone which provides a lighter sound than the seventh - experiment with using it in your own solos! Here is the slow demo and backing track:

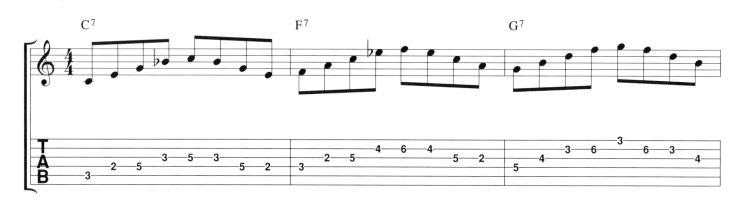

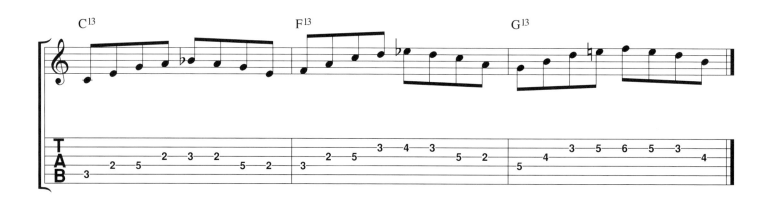

And here is the same exercise at full speed.

Slurs - Hammer-ons, Pull-offs and Slides

We've given a lot of emphasis throughout this book to scales and arpeggios, which may seem quite academic - however, it will only take a small amount of experimentation before these tools become useful musically.

Get into messing about with this information without getting bogged down in theory - just a little time spent with tools like this will explode your playing potential!

The next example will give you an opportunity to practise three different kinds of slurs - hammer-ons, pull-offs and slides. Use the slow backing track, making sure that you practise all these devices rhythmically - there's a real tendency to rush them!

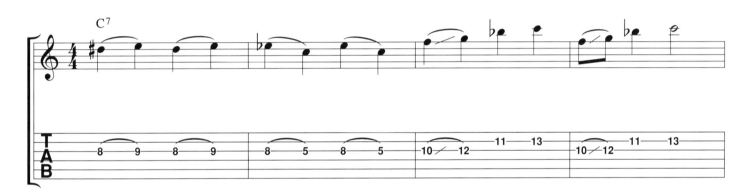

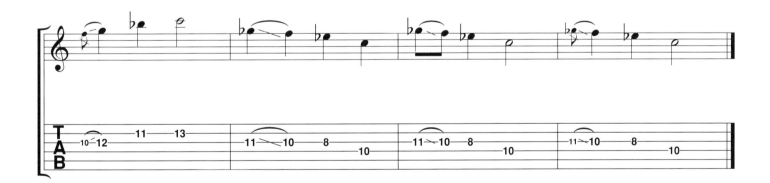

Once you're confident that your rhythm is rock steady try the same exercise at full speed.

Robben's Bag

If you've practised all the examples in this chapter you will now be ready to tackle the full solo!

This solo has a conversational feel - it flows rhythmically, with plenty of breathing spaces. Listen to how the great blues players use space - you'll be surprised at how little they actually play.

Note that the track starts with a drum roll rather than a count-in. Once you've mastered this solo, use some of the techniques and patterns in this chapter to improvise your own solo.

TRACKS 68+69

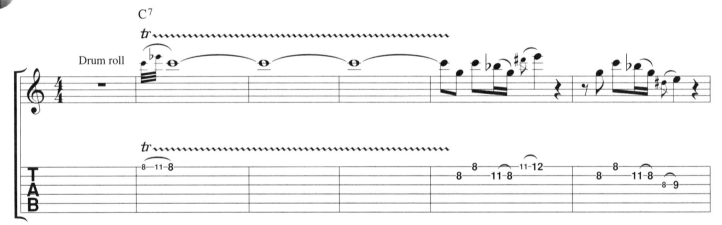

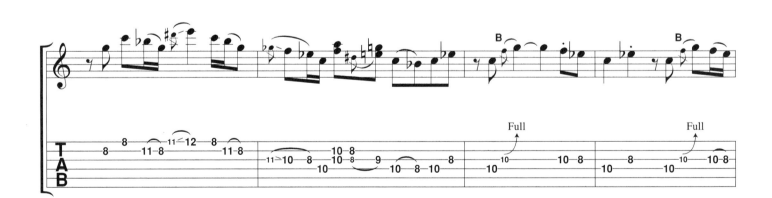

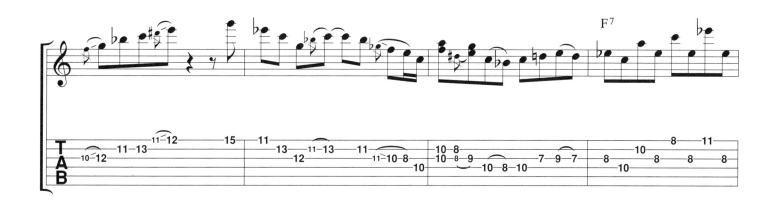

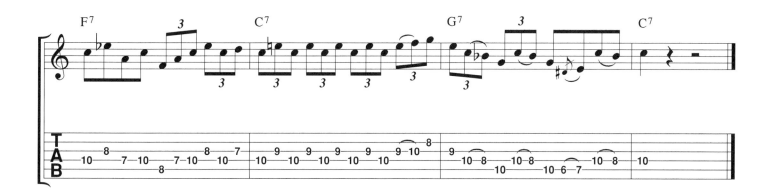

▶▶ Spotlight On Techniques

Trill:-

The track opens with a long trill - a hammer-on/pull off from C to E flat. This is a dramatic way to start any solo!

Repetitive Ideas:-

The three bars after the trill use a simple rhythmic motif with slight variations. The use of familiar material helps give the solo focus - and gives the listener something to hang on to.

Triplets:-

Towards the end of the track, the solo breaks into 1/8th note triplets, adding a little pace for an impressive finish. Don't be afraid to improvise using rhythms which contradict the underlying pulse - as time goes on your knowledge of music and strength of concentration will improve beyond belief.

▶▶ *BUDDY GUY*
    ...whose style combined classic Chicago Blues with contemporary soul styles, worked with artists spanning the spectrum of Blues, from Junior Wells and Howlin' Wolf to Eric Clapton and Mark Knopfler.

The Ali Shuffle
String Bending

The last tune is a blues shuffle played over a
seriously groovy drum pattern. The term shuffle
means that the piece has an underlying 1/8th
note triplet feel - just listen to the drum groove!

To start with, let's take a look at the technique of
string-bending - one of the fundamentals of
blues guitar playing. This example presents some
simple bends into chord tones, finishing with a
standard blues scale based lick. Listen really
carefully to make sure that the note you are
bending up to is exactly in tune.
Practise slowly ....

 **TRACKS 70+71**

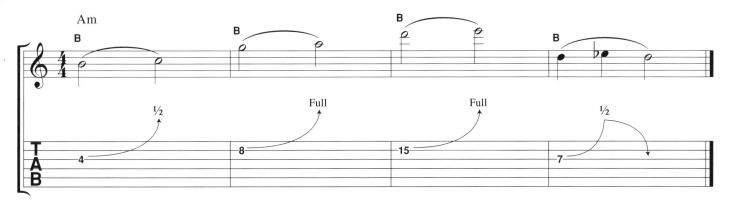

 **TRACKS 72+73**

... and then up to speed.

Grace-note Pre-bends

Now let's try some faster "grace-note" bends, which demand a swift movement. As always, start slowly and build up speed gradually.

TRACKS 74+75

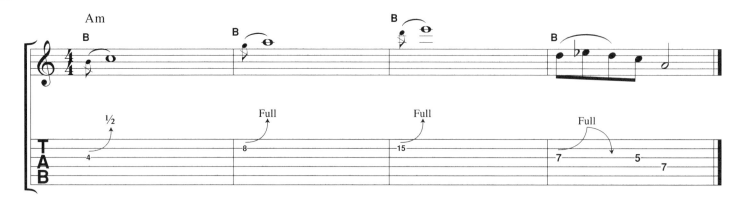

TRACKS 76+77

Here's the same example at full speed.

The next example introduces a "pre-bend" in bar 3 - you'll need to bend the string quickly before you strike it and then release the bend in time.

Once again, listen very carefully to make sure that all the bends are in tune.
Here's a slow version for practice...

TRACKS 78+79

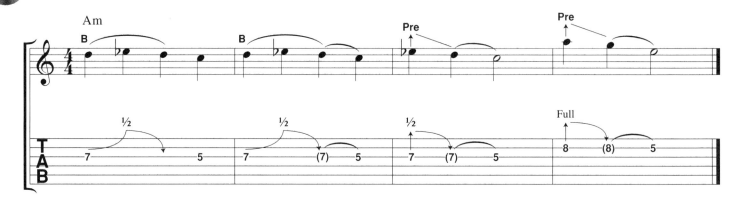

TRACKS 80+81

... and a version at full speed.

Double-stops With Bends

Finally, let's have a look at some double-stops
featuring bends - take care to distinguish
between the full tone bend and the quarter-tone
bend. Here's the example slowly ....

TRACKS 82+83

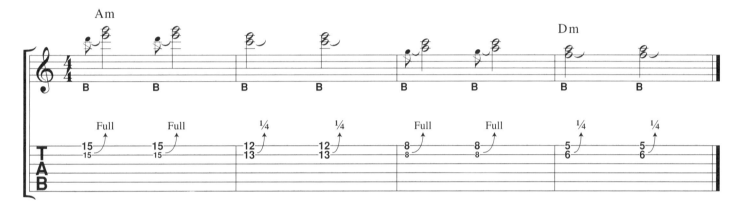

TRACKS 84+85

... and at speed.

▶▶ *T-BONE WALKER*
   *...whose showmanship, including playing guitar behind his head while doing
   the splits, later influenced artists such as Chuck Berry and Jimi Hendrix.*

Play The Blues!

All the techniques and patterns in this chapter are brought together in this final flowing solo - it's peppered with useful shapes and ideas. Learn the part as tabbed out here and then have a go at improvising your own solo.

▶▶Spotlight On Techniques

Triplets vs. Even Rhythms:-

This solo makes extensive use of both triplets and even subdivisions - listen to Track 86 if you're unsure of any of the rhythms.

Higher Register Playing:-

The improvisation opens with a roaring double stop played high up the instrument. You've paid for those frets at the 'dusty end' so use them! Exploring the extreme high and low registers can produce great results.

Quarter Tone Bends:-

Check out the use of 1/4 tone bends in this solo. These bends add another quality to the solo when used on the minor third (e.g. bar 7).

▶ **ALBERT KING**
"Albert King. Boy, now he played the blues! He's my favourite guitar player."
- John Lee Hooker

The Ali Shuffle

TRACKS 86+87

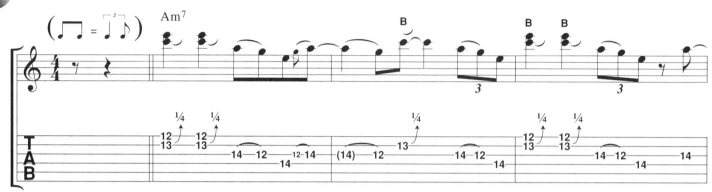

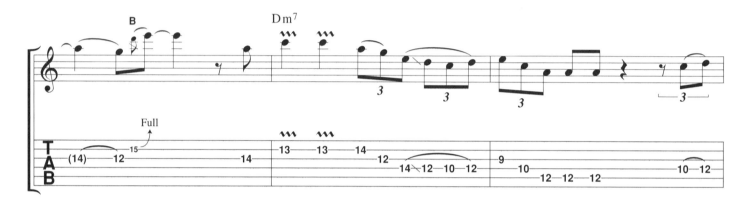

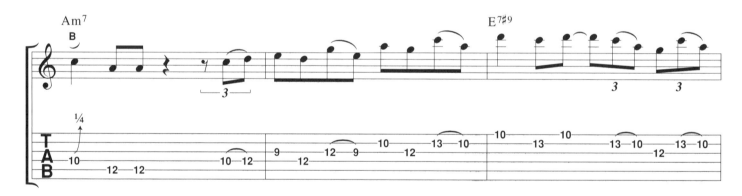

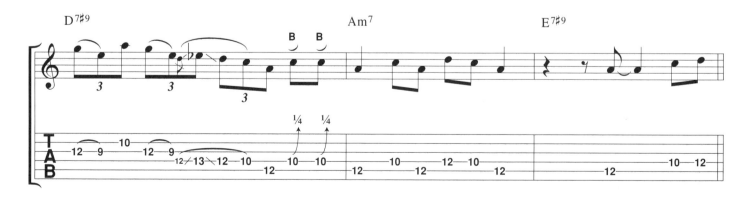

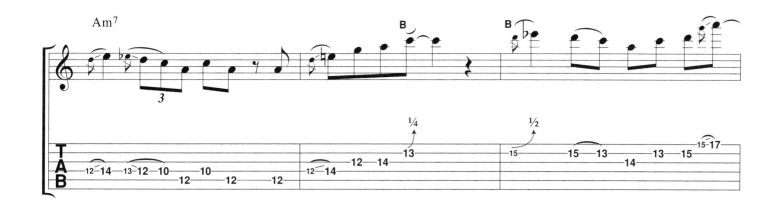

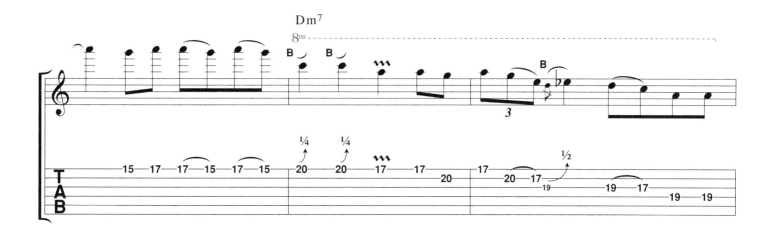

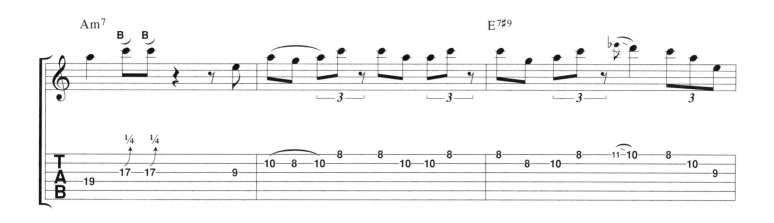

Congratulations !

The solos and examples in this book will give you all the raw materials you need to play great blues solos in any style. Take some time to listen to the demonstration solos as well as playing over the backing tracks - you should aim to absorb some of the style of playing, as well as getting the notes right.

Spend some time listening to some of the great American blues players - Albert King, Albert Collins, Johnny Winter, B.B. King, Buddy Guy, Stevie Ray Vaughan, Robben Ford and Jimi Hendrix. You may not be a virtuoso, but you can learn a lot about phrasing, melody and feel, just by listening to classic blues tracks.

Take any opportunity to play with other musicians - ALWAYS say yes to a gig or a rehearsal. If you want to explore further into the world of blues guitar, check out some of these other books from the Music Sales catalogue:

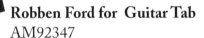

Original B.B. King
AM63504
Includes transcriptions of his most celebrated solos.

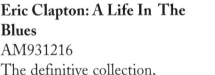

Robben Ford for Guitar Tab
AM92347
Ten classic songs in easy-to-read guitar tab and standard notation.

Eric Clapton: A Life In The Blues
AM931216
The definitive collection, featuring tab arrangements, photos, a biography and discography.

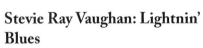

Stevie Ray Vaughan: Lightnin' Blues
HLE00660058
25 songs from five albums: *Texas Flood, Couldn't Stand the Weather, Soul to Soul, Live Alive* and *Back to the Beach*. Also includes section on his guitar style.

FastForward Blues Guitar
AM951160

FastForward Classic Blues Guitar Licks
AM92451

Part of the FastForward series. Everything you need to know to help you perfect your blues guitar technique!

Beginning Fingerstyle Blues Guitar
AM71390 (Book and CD)

Bottleneck Blues Guitar
OK64984

Acoustic Blues Guitar
HLE00000157